# GAME DAY
# Nice Hit!
## You Can Play Baseball

by Nick Fauchald

illustrated by Bill Dickson

Thanks to our advisers for their expertise, research, and advice:

Wendy Frappier, Ph.D.
Assistant Professor, Health and Physical Education Department
Minnesota State University, Moorhead, Minnesota

Susan Kesselring, M.A., Literacy Educator
Rosemount-Apple Valley-Eagan (Minnesota) School District

PICTURE WINDOW BOOKS
Minneapolis, Minnesota

Managing Editor: Bob Temple
Creative Director: Terri Foley
Editor: Brenda Haugen
Editorial Adviser: Andrea Cascardi
Copy Editor: Laurie Kahn
Designer: Nathan Gassman
Page production: Picture Window Books
The illustrations in this book are watercolor.

Picture Window Books
5115 Excelsior Boulevard
Suite 232
Minneapolis, MN 55416
1-877-845-8392
www.picturewindowbooks.com

Printed in the United States of America.

**Library of Congress Cataloging-in-Publication Data**
Fauchald, Nick.
Nice Hit!:You can play baseball / written by Nick Fauchald ; illustrated by Bill
Dickson.
p. cm.—(Game Day)
Includes bibliographical references (p.     ) and index.  Summary: A brief
introduction to the game of baseball as intended to be played by children.
ISBN 1-4048-0259-2 (hardcover)
ISBN 1-4048-0510-9 (paperback)
1.  Baseball Juvenile literature. [1. Baseball.]  I. Dickson, Bill, 1949- ill. II. Title.
GV867.5 .F38 2004
796.357—dc22                                                    2003019636

Baseball is played by millions of children all across the world. It is so popular, it is called America's favorite pastime. Teams try to score runs by hitting the baseball and running around the bases. If you can touch all four bases without getting out, you score a run. The team with the most runs at the end of the game wins.

It's a sunny Saturday afternoon—a perfect day to play baseball. Your teammate Maria stops by on her bike so you can ride to the field together.

You are so excited, you almost forget your glove on the kitchen table!

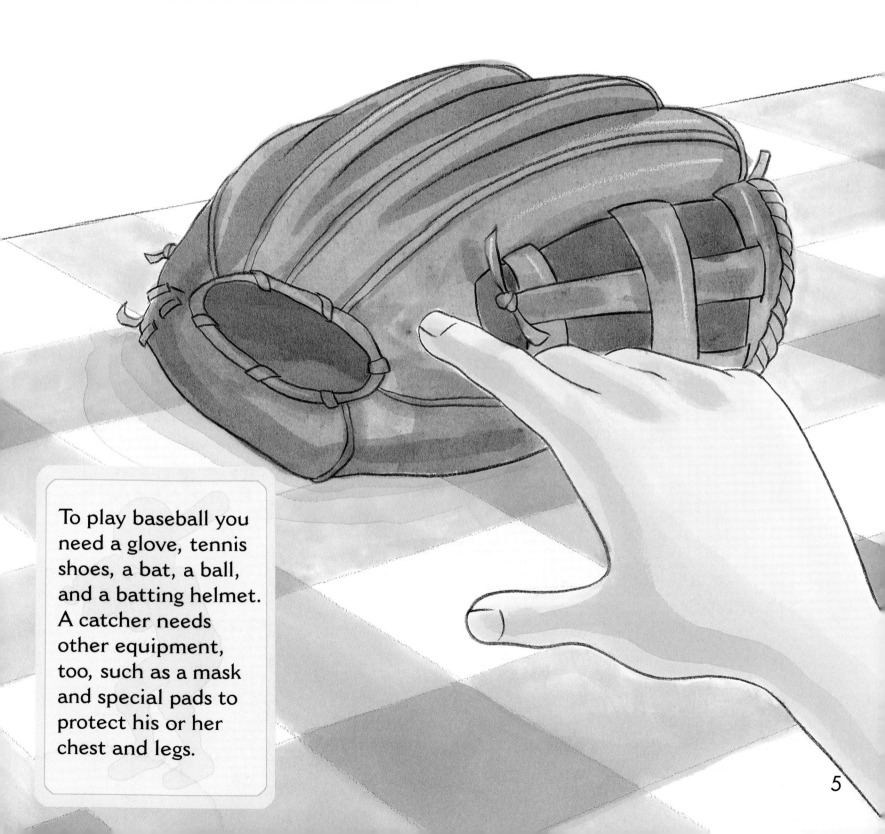

To play baseball you need a glove, tennis shoes, a bat, a ball, and a batting helmet. A catcher needs other equipment, too, such as a mask and special pads to protect his or her chest and legs.

When you get to the field, you and the other
Blue Jays warm up by playing catch.

Each team uses nine players in the field. The first, second, and third basemen stand near their bases. The outfielders stand a distance behind these infielders. The catcher squats behind home plate. The pitcher stands in the middle of the infield. The shortstop plays between second and third bases.

Maria stands on first base
and throws the ball to Karl
at second base. Cassie, the catcher,
waits for the next throw.

7

"Let's play ball!" your coach shouts. The Orioles, the visiting team, bat first. The first batter hits a ball high into the air.

Maria looks up at the sky and follows the ball as it starts to come down. She holds her arms up and watches the ball land in her glove. Nice catch!

Use both hands when catching. Hold your glove hand up, and put your free hand beside it. When the ball hits your glove, squeeze the glove shut, and cover it with your free hand. This will keep the ball from falling out.

9

**CRACK!** The next Orioles batter hits a ground ball to Maria at first base.

A game has six or more innings. In an inning, both teams get to bat until they get three outs.

Maria scoops up the ball and steps on first base before the hitter can get there. The hitter is out!

The next Oriole hits the ball past the infield and runs safely to first base. On the next pitch, the batter hits a ground ball right to Karl.

When you catch, or field, a ground ball, bend your knees and open your glove on the ground. Get in front of the ball, and watch it as it comes to you. Remember to use both hands to field the ball.

Karl bends down to field the ball before he tags the runner coming from first base. Three outs!

It's now the Blue Jays' turn to bat. You get to bat first,

so you put on your helmet. Here comes the pitch.

You swing at it.

When you swing at a pitch, make sure to keep your eyes on the ball. After you hit the ball, run to first base as fast as you can. If you make it there before somebody touches you or the base while holding the ball, you are safe.

You hit the ball past the third baseman. You drop the bat and run to first base. You are safe!

WHACK!

It is Karl's turn to bat. He hits the ball high into the air. The ball bounces before anyone can catch it.

You run to second base, and Karl makes it safely to first.
**"Nice hit,"** your coach says.

Maria brings her bat to the plate and gets ready to hit.

You get ready to run to third base.

**CRACK!** Maria hits a fly ball into the outfield. When the ball bounces on the ground, you start running toward third base.

If you are on base when the ball is hit, wait to see if anyone catches it. If someone does, the batter is out. *After* a catch is made, you can "tag up," or wait for the catch, and then run to the next base. But make sure the ball has been hit far enough away so you can make it to the next base safely.

As you touch third base, coach shouts, **"Keep going!"** You keep running toward home plate.

20

The third baseman throws the ball to the catcher, but you touch home plate before the catcher can tag you. **You score!** The Blue Jays are ahead 1-0, but the game is far from done. **It's a great day to play baseball!**

# Key:
# Baseball Positions

| | | | | | |
|---|---|---|---|---|---|
| **P** | Pitcher | **C** | Catcher | **1B** | First baseman |
| **2B** | Second baseman | **SS** | Shortstop | **3B** | Third baseman |
| **LF** | Left fielder | **CF** | Center fielder | **RF** | Right fielder |
| **B** | Batter | **U** | Umpire | | |

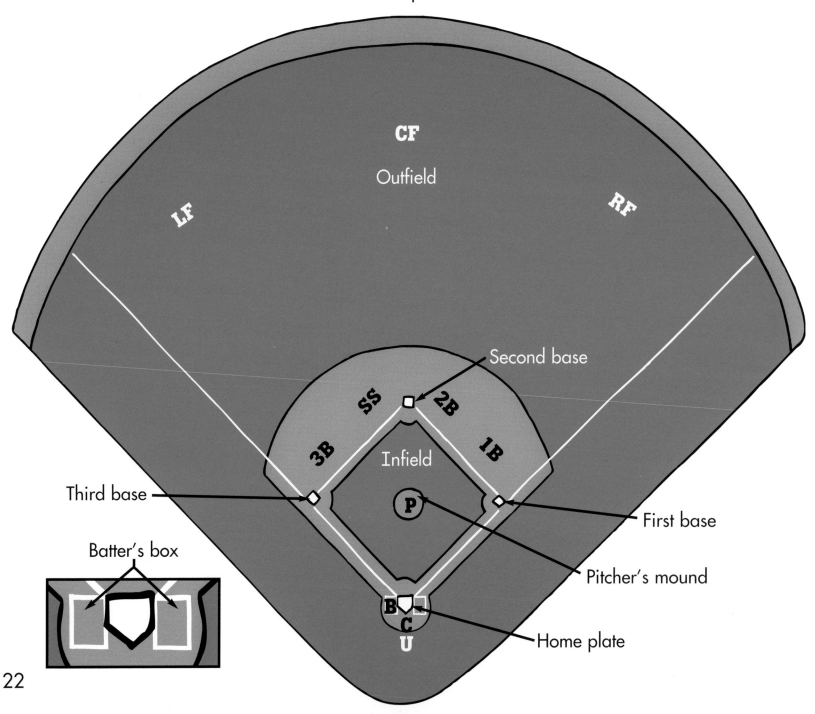

CF

Outfield

LF

RF

Second base

SS

2B

3B

1B

Infield

Third base

P

First base

Pitcher's mound

Batter's box

B

C

Home plate

U

22

## Fun Facts

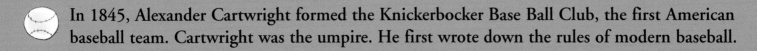

- In 1845, Alexander Cartwright formed the Knickerbocker Base Ball Club, the first American baseball team. Cartwright was the umpire. He first wrote down the rules of modern baseball.

- A woman has never played major league baseball, but there have been several women's professional leagues.

- In 1947, Jackie Robinson became the first African-American to play major league baseball. He played for the Brooklyn Dodgers.

- Major league baseballs have rubber centers wrapped tightly with twine. They are covered in white cowhide and stitched in a special way with red thread.

- Baseball became an Olympic sport in 1992. That year, the Olympics were held in Barcelona, Spain.

- The love of baseball started spreading throughout the United States during the Civil War. Union soldiers played baseball while Confederate prisoners watched. After the war, the Confederate soldiers taught others in the southern United States to play.

## Glossary

**fly ball**—a ball hit high in the air toward the outfield

**ground ball**—a ball that rolls or bounces along the ground after it is hit by the batter

**hit**—when a batter hits the ball and safely makes it to a base

**infield**—the area of a baseball field inside and including all four bases

**inning**—a part of a baseball game in which each team gets a turn to bat

**outfield**—the area of a baseball field behind first, second, and third bases

23

# To Learn More

## At the Library

Christopher, Matt. *The Lucky Baseball Bat.* Boston: Little, Brown, 1991.

Gibbons, Gail. *My Baseball Book.* New York: HarperCollins Publishers, 2000.

Kreutzer, Peter. *Little League's Official How-To-Play Baseball Book.* New York: Doubleday, 1990.

Silverstone, Michael. *Latino Legends: Hispanics in Major League Baseball.* Bloomington, Minn.: Red Brick Learning, 2004.

Smyth, Ian. *The Young Baseball Player.* New York: DK Pub., 1998.

## On the Web

Fact Hound offers a safe, fun way to find Web sites related to this book. All of the sites on Fact Hound have been researched by our staff.

1. Visit *www.facthound.com*

2. Type in this special code: 1404802592

3. Click on the FETCH IT button.

Your trusty Fact Hound will fetch the best sites for you!